OVERCOMING
BATTLES
OF THE
MIND

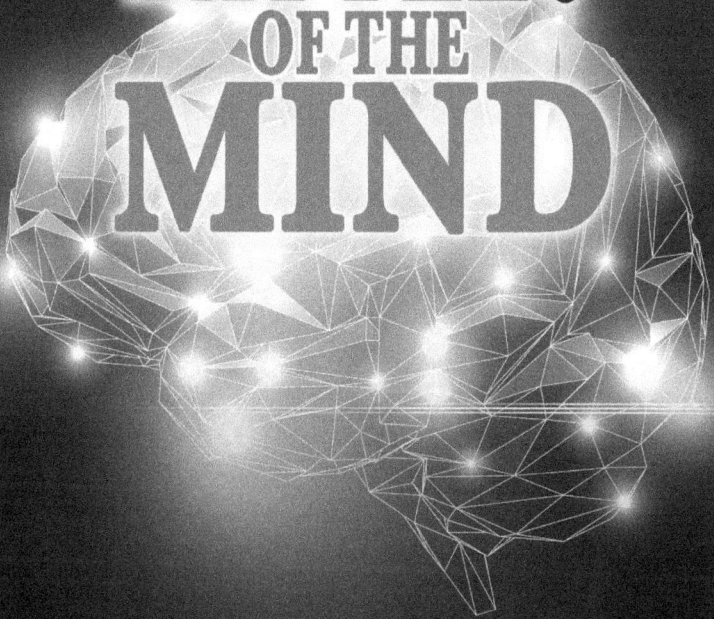

Developing Thinking Skills
For Effective Living

FESTUS ADEYEYE

OVERCOMING
BATTLES
OF THE
MIND

THE
CORNERSTONE
PUBLISHING

FESTUS ADEYEYE

OVERCOMING BATTLES OF THE MIND
Developing Thinking Skills For Effective Living
Copyright © 2015 by **Festus Adeyeye**

ISBN: 978-1-944652-05-0

Published By:
Cornerstone Publishing
Info@thecornerstonepublishers.com
www.thecornerstonepublishers.com
516.547.4999

Ordering Information:

To order books and tapes by Dr. Festus Adeyeye, please write to:
Dr. Festus Adeyeye
Adeyeye Evangelistic Ministries (AEM)
P.O Box 810
West Hempstead, NY 11552
E-mail: aboluade@aol.com
Website: www.alccwinnershouse.org

CONTENTS

INTRODUCTION

Congratulations as you pick up this piece of divinely inspired material that has been carefully put together in order to add value to your life. By reading this book, you are not just about to gather information, but you are also about to be impacted with divine revelations for your long awaited change. Irrespective of where you are or what is happening in your life at this moment, I sense in my spirit that the season of your life is about to change to a new and higher level. God is a level changer and a story changer!

This book is not just theoretical but very practical and is borne out of my experience as a spiritual life coach and mentor for several years. This has given me the opportunity to interact with different kinds of people over the years. Whenever things do not work the way we want, there are many people who are quick to change their environments, quick to change their jobs, or quick to change their spouses. I understand that there are times that you may need to change any of the above but changing any of them without first of all changing your ways of thinking will only result in temporary success. This book will equip you with the necessary wisdom, insight, and power to become the new you and also to master the most essential battles of life; battles of the mind.

All of the words on the pages of this book are strategic, divinely timed, and penned to accomplish a purpose. An abundance of prayers have gone into the production so you can find the courage and power to launch to your new level.

There are also seven potent breakthrough prayers for breaking strongholds seeking to control your mind at the end of the last chapter of this book. Praying those prayers will definitely help you break away from every form of addiction and destructive behavior.

I want you to say the following prayers as you begin to read this book:

Dear heavenly father, I thank you for where I am today and for the great future that lies ahead of me. I commit the next few moments to the Holy Spirit to guide me and to give me understanding as I read this book. I receive the grace not only to read, but to be able to practically apply the truth into my life for necessary changes. I rebuke any form of distraction that may seek to interfere with this process, in Jesus name.

UNDERSTANDING MENTAL WARFARE

CHAPTER 1

UNDERSTANDING MENTAL WARFARE

Most Christians only understand spiritual warfare as it relates to the forces of darkness and demonic manifestations, with little or no knowledge of how it relates to the mind. However, while it is indeed necessary that every Christian should be aware of the forces of darkness and how to fully deploy spiritual ammunitions to resist the devil, it is equally essential to be cognizant of the battles of the mind.

"For though we walk in the flesh, we do not war according to the flesh. For the weapons of our warfare are not carnal but mighty in God for pulling down strongholds, casting down arguments and every high

thing that exalts itself against the knowledge of God, bringing every thought into captivity to the obedience of Christ" (2 Corinthians 10:3-5).

The above scripture introduces us to another dimension of spiritual warfare that is often unknown and neglected, namely, mental spiritual warfare. This is the battle that rages on in the mind of every individual. It is absolutely impossible to enjoy any lasting progress without first mastering this dimension of warfare.

WHY YOU MUST WIN

As you journey through life, there is always a contention for the control of your life; your mind is therefore, a battleground. Whatever controls your mind controls your life. If fear dominates and controls your mind, faith and victory will elude you. If anxiety and apprehension control your mind, you will be bound within the confines of the invisible wall created by these forces, and living a life of unlimited possibilities will elude you.

On the flip side, if your mind is filled with faith and possibilities, fear will fade away. If your mind is saturated with the fullness of God's grace and word, you will be filled with strength and courage.

If you win the battles of the mind, you have won the battles of life. Progress and breakthrough cannot be achieved beyond the level of the control you have over your mind. If the mind is sick, the whole body is sick. If the mind is well, the whole body will be well.

NATURE OF THE BATTLE

The battle of the mind is not physical; it is unseen and thus cannot be fought physically. Your mind is constantly bombarded with dangerous and poisonous thoughts. It is said that an average of four thousand thoughts pass through the mind daily. This is why the Scripture counsels:

> *"Above all, taking the shield of faith with which you will be able to quench all the fiery darts of the wicked one. And take the helmet of salvation, and the sword of the Spirit, which is the word of God"* (Ephesians 6:16-17).

Thoughts can be good or bad, positive or negative. Bad or negative thoughts are what the above scripture refers to as the fiery darts of the wicked. A thought that is not taken captive upon entering someone's mind will become an imagination. The imagination state is when the person begins to weave the thought into images. If the thought is not dealt with at this stage, it grows into a stronghold.

WHAT IS A STRONGHOLD?

A stronghold is when a poisonous thought has established dominion in the mind. A stronghold therefore, is not a demon trying to afflict you but a poisonous thought targeted at robbing you of your place in destiny.

Satan did not send a witch to Adam and Eve in the Garden of Eden; rather, he penetrated and manipulated their minds through deceptive thoughts. Every form of addiction or wrong behavior always commences as a thought before progressing to an imagination and later a stronghold.

A stronghold is when a person automatically manifests certain actions or behaviors. In other words, thoughts that have become strongholds require little or no effort on someone's part for them to manifest.

Negative or bad thoughts that have become strongholds often manifest as destructive behavioral tendencies. For instance, it is possible for a pregnant woman to be saturated with the thoughts of premature birth or the delivery of an abnormal child. A sick person can be filled with the thoughts of death, instead of healing.

PRACTICAL EXPERIENCES

My wife and I ministered to a sister five years ago, who always had thoughts of stabbing her husband and children with a kitchen knife whenever they were asleep. When exposed to the truth of God's word and was led in series of deliverance prayers, she gained victory over the oppressive thoughts. She gained the understanding that the thoughts were satanic in origin and was taught how to prayerfully take her thoughts captive. The family has since been flourishing and experiencing the wonders of God's abiding presence.

Some time ago, my wife brought a lady into my office and did something unusual. She asked what I thought of the lady's appearance. At first, I didn't know what to make of the question; then I understood her intention. I replied in all sincerity that the lady looked very beautiful as a daughter of God. It was then that my wife explained to me that the same lady had contemplated suicide several times, simply because she kept entertaining the negative thought that she was ugly.

That destructive stronghold was formed in the beautiful young lady because a parental authority repeatedly told her, while growing up, that she was a good-for-nothing ugly child. That thought became dominant in her mind and gave room for the devil to keep oppressing her. Thank God that we were able to prayerfully set her free through the power of God and His word.

It is very important to understand how Satan uses poisonous thoughts (fiery darts) to establish strongholds in people's minds. This will not only safeguard us against his manipulations (2 Corinthians 2:11), but will also equip us with the knowledge we need to help others.

MASTERING YOUR THOUGHTS

CHAPTER 2

MASTERING YOUR THOUGHTS

There is a saying that you may not be able to prevent a bird from flying over your head, but you can prevent it from building a nest on your head. You may not be able to prevent a thought from coming into your mind, but you can surely prevent it from gaining control of your mind.

Listed below are six ways to handle your thoughts so you can enjoy a life of consistent victory.

1. Take Your Thought Life Seriously.

By reason of ignorance, many people just go through life, ignoring the way they think or their thought pattern in general. Some even pay more attention to the devil than the thoughts they allow in their minds. I am not suggesting that you ignore the devil; but you must also of necessity be mindful of the thoughts you allow to gain access into your mind.

The mind is like the storage device inside the computer. Whatever you save in it will be there as long as the computer works. Every event you witness, every word you hear or every picture you see registers on your mind. Therefore, you must be deliberate about what you allow or disallow into your mind.

2. Realize that Not Every Thought Comes From God.

Thoughts can come from three sources: God, Satan and your environment. So, the first thing to always do is to discern the thought that comes into your mind. This is so you can determine the source, which will reveal the intention of the thought. It is possible to embrace negative thoughts or suggestions with the mistaken impression that God is the one speaking to you.

Here is the litmus test that will help you to properly discern the origin of any thought that comes into your mind. You must know that the spirit of God will never suggest that you do what is contradictory to God's word. Also, Satan will never ask you to do anything that is in alignment with God's word. Satan can sometimes pervert the word of God and make it appear as if it is God speaking so he, Satan can deceive you. That was exactly what he did to Eve in the Garden of Eden; but if you pay careful attention, you will discern the difference.

> *"Now the serpent was more cunning than any beast of the field which the LORD God had made. And he said to the woman, "Has God indeed said, 'You shall not eat of every tree of the garden?'" And the woman said to the serpent, 'We may eat of the fruit of the trees of the garden;...For God knows that in the day you eat of it your eyes will be opened, and you will be like God, knowing good and evil"* (Genesis 3:1-2, 5).

If you carefully examine the statement above, it started with the planting of doubt of what God said in the mind of Eve. "Has God indeed said…?" Satan made this statement so Eve could begin to doubt the authenticity or validity of the word of God. Then he followed with an inaccurate restatement of what God said; "You shall not eat of every tree of the garden." God instruction to them was not to eat of a particular tree, not all of the trees. Satan said this with the intention of confusing Eve's mind.

"Then the serpent said to the woman, "You will not surely die" (Genesis 3:4).

The ultimate intention is to cause you to disbelieve God's instruction for your life. For example it is possible for Satan to suggest lies into someone's mind that taking narcotics or destructive drugs will have no adverse consequences. If embraced, the above may be the beginning of a life of addiction. Similarly, he may lie to a person through suggestions that romance outside of the marital home has no adverse consequences. When embraced, that may lead to a life of deceit and adultery in the marital home that could ultimately lead to the breakdown of that marriage. Always remember that God will never suggest to you or ask you to do anything that is contradictory to His word.

3. Understand that the Associations, Information, and Teachings You are Exposed to Influence Your Thoughts.

There are certain places you should not go, certain music you must not listen to, and certain negative information, you should not feed your mind.

Avoid any gathering or association that fills your mind with unbelief or doctrines that are unbiblical. Instead, deliberately position yourself where you can hear, see and observe faith-filled positive words.

4. Renounce, Rebuke, and Resist Negative Thoughts.

When negative thoughts come to your mind, don't entertain them; instead, quickly subject such thoughts to the word of God through the filter of faith in your mind.

Judge all thoughts with the word of God to determine whether they are in consonant with it. If not, such thoughts should be brought into alignment with the word of God (2 Corinthians 10:3-5).

Harmful thoughts that are contrary to the word of God should be rejected, rebuked, and renounced in prayer. Locate specific scriptures that counteract the areas where Satan attacks you and confess the word of God that addresses such situations.

For instance, if as a pregnant woman, you're filled with thoughts of premature delivery, such oppressive thoughts should be renounced, using God's promises like, *"No one shall suffer miscarriage or be barren in your land..."* (Exodus 23:26). Or if you suddenly receive a thought that you are worthless and inferior to others, you can repeatedly confess the word of God in Psalms 139:14: *"I will praise You, for I am fearfully and wonderfully made…* " You can also prayerfully confess the word of God in Colossians 2:10 that says, "You are complete in Him [Christ]."

Since you are wonderfully made and are complete in Christ, it means that you are neither inferior nor worthless; you are a creature of inestimable value. Keep confessing these scriptures in prayer and worship until the negative thoughts are expelled.

It is advisable to take at least one day a week to fast and prayerfully focus on the specific area of challenge. Fasting keeps your flesh under so that the spirit man can gain control.

5. Deliberately and Prayerfully Refuse to Give any Negative Thought a Voice.

When a negative thought comes to your mind, you must deliberately and prayerfully refuse to give it a voice. Every thought is seeking a voice to express and manifest itself as an experience. So, one of the easiest ways to reject and defeat a negative thought is to deny the thought with your voice. Do not voice the thought; instead, speak the word of God that addresses such a situation out loud, with conviction.

"Casting down imaginations, and every high thing that exalteth itself against the knowledge of God, and

bringing into captivity every thought to the obedience of Christ" (2 Corinthians 10:5, KJV).

Every time an evil thought comes to your mind, instead of voicing it, simply declare: "I cast you out in Jesus name!"

6. Continue to Fine-Tune Your Mind With the Word Of God, Daily.

"Finally, brethren, whatever things are true, whatever things are noble, whatever things are just, whatever things are pure, whatever things are lovely, whatever things are of good report, if there is any virtue and if there is anything praiseworthy - meditate on these things" (Philippians 4:8).

You become what you behold. What you dwell on is what you become. Satan will do anything to keep you away from the word. When you are hot, you cannot be hurt. But when the fire goes down, danger looms.

Proverbs 4:23 says, *"Above all else, guard your heart, for everything you do flows from it" (NIV).* Your heart is the center of your thoughts. The word heart here is interchangeably used for the mind. Your mind is the root of every thought and action that flow from you.

Satan only occupies vacant places. On each of the

occasions that he came to tempt Jesus, Jesus confronted him with the word. Whenever we receive the word of God into our hearts, we also receive His nature, which is the nature of boldness, victory and breakthrough. Our minds are also refocused and renewed.

The quantity of God's word in you determines the size of your mind and the size of your mind determines the size of your life. If your mind is small, your life will be small. There are certain things that I can attempt and achieve today that I couldn't attempt to attain in the past because of the limited amount of God's word that I had in my mind.

When you expand the size of your mind, you will see how small your problem is. God wants you to think big, think prosperous, think victorious, think honorable, think blessed, and think favored. You have to be deliberate about altering your mind and making it align with the word of God. Change your mentality from the way the world thinks, so that you won't go through the pain the world goes through. (Deuteronomy 8:3).

As you feed on the truths of God's word, you develop possibility-mentality because, as I said before, you become what you behold!

YOUR MIND, YOUR ASSET

CHAPTER 3

YOUR MIND, YOUR ASSET

"For as he thinks in his heart, so is he" (Proverbs 23:7).

The ability to use your mind correctly is one of your greatest assets in life. The height of success you attain, your ability to move forward to the next level, your general pursuits in life, the things you allow or disallow, what you consider unimportant or valuable, your response to crisis, and how you handle opportunities are all based on the way you think.

There are several new revelations, new ideas and new levels that God wants you to experience in this season. Indeed, God is constantly seeking to do new things in your life, settling your past, resolving your present and securing your future. Your mind must however be able to comprehend and embrace His moves.

The Israelites could not enter into God's provision of a flourishing land because of wrong thinking. There is nothing like bad luck for a child of God but there can be a bad mind. So, we need to change the way we think in order to move higher beyond our current level to higher levels.

Do you desire a new level in your health? Do you desire a new level financially? Do you desire a new level in your career? Or do you desire a new level in your relationship? You must upgrade your thinking.

POWER OF YOUR THOUGHT

As a person thinks so he becomes. So, thinking is a process of becoming something. The thinking process of a person is instrumental to the manifestation of that person's personality.

You are where you are today as a result of (your) yesterdays decisions which emanated from (your) yesterdays thoughts; what you think today is what you will become hereafter. In other words, the way you think affects your decision-making, which will ultimately determine your accomplishments in life.

Someone once said that there are no rich or poor people - we only have people with either rich or poor minds. You cannot have a poor mind and a rich hand. God brought an entire generation of the Israelites out of Egypt with the intention of taking them into a flourishing land; sadly, however, their carcasses ended up littering the wilderness because of wrong and inferior thinking, known as the "grasshopper mentality."

While God saw the Israelites as possessor of lands and territories, they saw themselves as inferior slaves and possessors of nothing. They saw themselves as grasshoppers. Only Caleb and Joshua chose to think differently, and they were the only ones in that generation to enter into the Promised Land (Numbers 14:6-24).

I dare you to see yourself as God sees you today. You are not a loser but a winner. Did you just fail in a business or your career? That does not make you a failure. Don't allow the spirit or mindset of failure to grip you.

It is your thinking that creates your reality. It can create possibilities and opportunities, or limitations and boundaries that are not even in existence. John Milton, in his 1866 poem, Paradise Lost, says in line 254-255:

"The mind is its own place, and in itself can make a Heaven of hell, a hell of Heaven." This means that the mind is so powerful that even when you are in a heaven-like situation, your mind can make it seem like a hellish situation. Similarly, when you are in a hellish situation, your mind can create heaven out of it. It is therefore very crucial that you learn how to think correctly in order to fully deploy your potentials and embrace the best of life.

CONTENT OF YOUR THOUGHT

"For as he thinks in his heart, so is he." (Proverbs 23:7)

Everybody is doing one form of thinking or the other in life. You are either thinking good or evil. You are either thinking progress or failure. You are either thinking wealth or poverty. Your brain can never be in the neutral. Your ability to channel your energy into thinking positively and meaningfully is what determines whether you are successful or not.

Irrespective of the barrier confronting you, God has given you the ability to think your way through. The word of God is so clear and definite: "As a man thinks in his mind so is he." So you are not always the product of your environment or circumstances but the exact

32

product of your thinking.

As a matter of fact, you can change your environment and your circumstances with the way you think. According to Winston Churchill, *"the empires of the future are the empires of the mind."* You will only build your world according to your mindset.

YOUR THOUGHT AND YOUR WORLD

There are many people who think change will automatically occur when they change their environment. When a marriage seems not to be working, many are quick to change their spouses. However, changing your spouse without changing the way you think does not guarantee a good second marriage.

Changing a neighborhood without changing the way you think will only recreate the same neighborhood you just left. Someone who has a toxic mind will invariably have a toxic marriage. A poor mind will produce a poor life. Conversely, a rich and great mind will produce great relationships.

A person who lives in a two-bedroom apartment that is often unkempt and stuffed with junk may move into a six-bedroom house and still have difficulty keeping it tidy, if the mind is not renewed. The same mind that produced the mess in the previous apartment will reproduce the same mess in the new environment.

It often amazes me when I look at certain neighborhoods in America with predominant immigrant groups. The neighborhood soon changes to look like the country of origin of the predominant immigrants. For instance, you see people hawking foods in neighborhoods of immigrants that come from countries where food is hawked on the street.

If people in an undeveloped country and those in a developed country were to swap locations for 20 years, I am sure that both groups would soon turn their new countries into the same conditions as their previous ones. This has nothing to do with the weather, resources or locations of the countries; it is about the mentalities of the different groups of people.

What this implies therefore is that in order to enjoy lasting success, the change you desire in every area of your life must begin from your mind. If you change your thinking, your income level will change. If you change your thinking, your health will change. If you change your thinking, your earning power will change.

We have a great assurance in Ephesians 3:20 that God is able to do far exceedingly, abundantly more than we can ask or think. What this means is that the way you think determines how God works in your life. God's ability in your life is in accordance with both your asking and thinking.

Also, in Genesis 11:6, we're told:

> *"And the Lord said, Behold, the people is one, and they have all one language; and this they begin to do: and now nothing will be restrained from them, which they have imagined to do"* (KJV).

God testifies here to the fact that no one can stop you from achieving whatever you have rooted inside of your mind. If you feed your mind with the thought of your next dimension, no one can stop you from attaining it. I see you going to the top in Jesus name.

YOUR MIND, YOUR EYES

CHAPTER 4

YOUR MIND, YOUR EYES

Have you ever considered this truth? Although you look with your eyes, you don't really see with your eyes but with your mind. So, your mind is your true "organ" of vision.

Genesis 13:14-15 says,

"And the Lord said to Abram, after Lot had separated from him: "Lift your eyes now and look from the place where you are - northward, southward, eastward, and westward; for all the land which you see I give to you and your descendants forever."

Abraham, who was well over 75 years, couldn't have

been able to see too far with his physical eyes. So, God wasn't referring only to the land which his physical eyes could see. God was actually referring to what Abraham could see with his mind. He was going to have as far as his mind could see and grasp.

God was simply asking Abraham to think and visualize His plans for him. The reason is because, for God's plans to be made manifest in Abraham's life, his mind must be able to conceive them. What this denotes is that we don't usually see and interpret things the way they are but the way our minds want them to appear.

PERCEPTION AND MANIFESTATION

Stephen Covey was right when he said, *"We see the world, not as it is, but as we are."* Similarly, Dr. A.R. Barnard, Senior Pastor of the Christian Cultural Center, New York, once made this striking remark during one of his sermons: *"What you see is colored by the condition of your mind."*

This is a very profound statement. It means that if I am small-minded, I will see everything around me as small. If I am scarcity-minded, I will only see lack even in the midst of abundance. If I am slavery-minded I will see the whole world as a prison trying to hold me back and thus see everyone taking advantage of me. If I am simple-minded, every problem will look too complex for me. If I am self-minded, I will expect favor and help from everyone around me, without willing to offer anything in return.

Things appear exactly the way you see them with your mind. The question is, what mental spectacles are you wearing? Everyone wears a shade of mental spectacles or goggles. So, what shade are you wearing? If you are wearing transparent spectacles, everything will be pure to you. If you are wearing defiled spectacles, everything will be defiled.

If you are wearing poverty spectacles, everything will appear poor even in the midst of plenty and opportunities. If you are wearing abundance and prosperity spectacles, everything will look prosperous even in the midst of lack and insufficiencies.

Essentially, it is a function of how you see and not so much how things are out there.

HOW THOUGHT INFLUENCES ACTION

Titus 1:15 confirms the connection between imagination and approach to life:

"Unto the pure all things are pure: but unto them that are defiled and unbelieving is nothing pure; but even their mind and conscience is defiled." (Titus 1:15, KJV)

Paul in 1 Corinthians 13:11 also says,

"When I was a child, I spake as a child, I understood as a child, I thought as a child: but when I became a man, I put away childish things." (KJV)

The above scriptures reveal that the state of your mind influences your actions. If you are in a state of purity, your actions and interpretations are going to be very pure. If you are in a state of depravity, everything you do will be depraved. When you are in a state of childishness, everything you do will be childish. If you are in a state of maturity, everything you do will reflect maturity.

When pure thoughts fill your mind, pure acts will be the result. When thoughts of prosperity fill your mind, financial abundance will be your experience. When healing thoughts fill your mind, health and wellness become your experience.

I once heard a message on this subject and the teacher used various shades of colored spectacles as example. He used bluish, yellowish and blackish shades. If one person wears different shades of spectacles in the same room, he or she will definitely see the room differently, depending on the shade he puts on. Although it is the same room, the person will see the room based on the shade of spectacles given. The point is that your thinking gives color to your mind, which determines how you see and interpret things.

THE ORPHANAGE
MENTALITY

CHAPTER 5

THE ORPHANAGE MENTALITY

I don't know if you have ever come across this expression but I find it very instructive and illustrative of the central message of this book. Before delving into it, however, let me quickly show you a few more truths about the mind.

Colossians 3:2 says, *"Set your mind on things above, not on things on the earth."*

A mindset is a mind that is set or conditioned in a certain way. If you pour concrete on a floor, you can move and mold it before it sets. However, the moment it sets, you cannot mold it because it would have hardened.

A person's mind can also become set in a certain way, thereby forming the basis by which the person sees and interprets life. The good thing about the mind, however, is that a mind that is set wrongly can be transformed and renewed through the word of God.

FACTS ABOUT MINDSET

- Your mindset is the way you SEE the world. We see things the way our minds have instructed our eyes to see them. We see things as we know them or as we want them to be.

- Your mindset is the way you UNDERSTAND things or the way you understand reality. I am sure that you have met some people whose ways of interpreting things just don't make sense. Their ways of doing things are not usually in consonance with reality; but to them it is normal. This is because their minds have been set to understand things wrongly.

- Your mindset is the way you RESPOND to things around you. What do you do when you are challenged? What do you do when you are faced with impossibility? Your response will always come from the standards you have given to your mind. "As a man thinks, so is he." So if your mind has been conditioned to fear, you will always respond in fear to every situation. If your mind has been conditioned to faith and possibilities in God, you will always respond in faith and hope in the ability of God.

A PECULIAR ORPHAN

My wife once told me the story of a young orphan who had lived in an orphanage for several years before being adopted by a rich couple. Soon after, his adoptive parents observed something intriguing about him. During meal times, the young boy would steal and stuff pieces of food in his clothes. The couple were baffled because there was usually abundant food on the dining table for him to eat freely. So why steal what belonged to him?

It was later the couple realized that during his stay at the orphanage, in order to have enough to eat, he had to scramble for food immediately it got to the dining table. This was due to insufficient supply of food at the orphanage. Ironically, now that the young boy had become the son of a very rich couple and was also rich by adoption, he still retained the thinking and attitude of an orphan. In other words, he was still being driven by the orphanage mentality of insufficiency and lack.

The unrenewed mind of the young orphan led to his action of stealing food from the dining table in his new home. What he needed was to have his mind retrained and realigned to adjust to his new status of abundance and prosperity.

Indeed, it is possible for a person to have progressed from a lifestyle of low living to a new status of affluence but still manifest a character that is inconsistent with the new status. Thus, he continues to manifest the characteristics of the former status of low living and associating with the wrong crowd from his past.

The level of thinking that brought you to where you are may not be able to take you beyond where you are. So, in order to transition properly to your next level, it is very crucial to embrace the mindset of the next level you desire.

FORMS OF MINDSET

Our minds can be set in either of two extreme positions. We can either be fixed-minded or double-minded.

A person is said to be fixed-minded when he has only one way of looking at an issue. With a fixed mindset, the person's position never changes, even in the face of disproving facts and truths. Of course there are certain positive areas of life in which we are required to have a fixed mindset, but it is essential to be able to discern such.

Sadly however, when a person has a fixed mind on something negative, he is unable to reason in any other way on the issue. For instance, some people have the mindset that women are inferior to men, and there is nothing anyone can say that can change their opinion. As Proverbs 27:22 says, *"Though you grind a fool in a mortar with a pestle along with crushed grain, Yet his foolishness will not depart from him."*

As I mentioned before, the other extreme of being fixed-minded is being double-minded. A double-minded person is often unable to have a definite view over an issue. People in this category are unstable in all their ways because they can't make up their minds. They are always joggling with different concepts, without being able to make up their minds. James 1:6-8 says of such people: *"...for he who doubts is like a wave of the sea driven and tossed by the wind. For let not that man suppose that he will receive anything from the Lord; he is a double-minded man, unstable in all his ways."*

SHADES OF DOUBLE-MINDEDNESS

Under the extreme mindset of double-mindedness, there are five sub-divisions that I would like to briefly talk about because of their significance. It was these shades of mindset that limited the Israelites and their progress in the journey to the Promised Land after being released from the Egyptians' captivity. You must avoid operating in these mindsets if you desire a life of progress and breakthrough.

1.   The slavery mindset. The Israelites were slaves in Egypt for over four hundred years, where they weren't able to act or think independently. The Egyptian system thought for them. The system governed all their actions and made decisions for them. They were conditioned to be absolutely dependent on the system for anything and everything. Consequently, after they had left Egypt, each time they encountered a problem, all they thought of was returning to Egypt, despite the fact that the system was oppressive.

People who have slavery mentality or mindset are usually bound to the control and opinions of other people. Such people would rather stay in an abusive situation than embrace the liberty and joy in Jesus Christ. They are always looking for solutions in the wrong places or people. Their language always reflects helplessness and hopelessness.

Someone who has the mindset of dependency cannot create anything. Such a person will continue to borrow until he is broke, even when he is in the midst of wealth. When people ask what the problem is, he will continue to say, "That is who I am" or "That is how things are." Eventually, he will begin to attribute his misery to the devil.

2. The scarcity mindset. The Israelites lived in scarcity for so long in Egypt that they were stuck in a mode of thinking that there was never enough. So, when God gave them the opportunity to gather manna for each day, they went and gathered more than necessary, thinking there would not be enough the next day.

Living under a prolonged life of scarcity and lack can cause someone to develop the mindset of scarcity. Growing up in Africa in my younger years, the common practice at the bus stop in big cities was for people to rush into any approaching mass transit bus. Even when there were many buses arriving, we had all conditioned our minds that there were no sufficient vehicles. So, we were always in a hurry to rush into the available ones.

You can overcome this mindset by understanding

53

that God, as your source, has made adequate provision for your destiny.

3. The simplicity mindset. The Israelites in Egypt weren't allowed by the system to develop any problem-solving skills because they were only deployed to do heavy physical work; they were never involved in the planning process. Thus, anytime problems arose, they didn't know what to do. After securing their liberty, anytime there was difficulty, they reacted hysterically. They complained about every little problem and responded with an attitude that reflected a simplistic point of view. At each point of challenge, they blamed Moses, who was helping them, as the source of their problem. They would rather go back to Egypt to suffer as slaves than to confront the challenges of entering and possessing their given lands.

The person with a simplicity mindset would rather scale back into a life of mediocrity than forge ahead to deploy his full potential. I challenge you to arise today and begin to embrace your God-given best.

4. The smallness mindset. The entire population of the Israelites was cramped into only a small section of town – Goshen - in Egypt. Millions were forced to live in a place designed for very few people. Accordingly, having lived in a small place for too long, they became contented with little, without the least appetite for more. In fact, many of them were never excited about the land flowing with milk and honey.

Small-minded people cannot see or embrace new opportunities. They have been conditioned never to expect more from life but to just stay within the status quo. A person with smallness mindset is easily excited and sedated by little success. They would rather remain small than aspire for greater or bigger things because big things blow their minds.

This smallness mindset must be changed because when you think small, you act small; when you believe small, you do small. The point is that when you have the mindset of smallness, you are easily satisfied.

No doubt, smallness can sometimes be beautiful. But when, for instance, you are doing a business that requires competition, smallness is not always good. In fact, in the business environment generally, smallness is not always smart because if you remain small, someone else will grow big and figuratively, swallow you up.

5. The selfish mindset. The language of the people with selfish mindset is often "What is in it for me?" They are always looking for people to do things for them and are never interested in doing anything for others. You are not rich until you become an outreach.

Your true measure of greatness does not lie in the amount of wealth you accumulate but in the lives you are able to positively impact.

THE RIGHT MINDSET

What God desires for you is to have a growth mind or what is known as the transformed mind. It is a mindset that is open to learn and can make adjustments where necessary.

A growth or transformed mind pursues growth and excellence.

Apostle Paul encourages us in Philippians 3:13-14 to adopt this mindset in the pursuit of excellence and effective living. Every Christian should always have the mindset that consistently rejects mediocrity and aspires to make progress to the next level, no matter the current level of achievement.

The transformed or growth mind only desires to become a God-pleaser, instead of a conformer to the dictates of the flesh. As Romans 12:2 says, *"And do not be conformed to this world, but be transformed by the renewing of your mind, that you may prove what is that good and acceptable and perfect will of God."*

This is easily achieved by replacing whatever errors are in our minds with the truth of God's words through biblical meditation.

THE ART OF BIBLICAL MEDITATION: CHANGING YOUR CORE BELIEFS

CHAPTER 6

THE ART OF BIBLICAL MEDITATION: CHANGING YOUR CORE BELIEFS

You think the way you do because of what you believe. It is your core beliefs that determine your behavior. Four things determine your core beliefs: Your environment, the people in your life, the information you are continually exposed to and your life experiences.

Upon their release from Egypt, the entire generation of the Israelites that came out of slavery couldn't embrace the provision of a flourishing land. Although they were already delivered from Egypt, their minds and thinking were still governed by the ways of life of the Egyptians.

SIGNIFICANCE OF MEDITATION

In order to have good and lasting success, we are encouraged to daily practice the art of meditation. This is a form of thinking that is based on godly counsel.

On the other hand, there is a form of thinking that is not based on the word of God. This "natural thinking" may allow you to prosper but will not give you good success. Natural thinking is based on worldly or natural logic. It is the thinking that is based only on the visible and not the invisible. It is a form of thinking that is based on accumulating valuables, rather than becoming valuable. This type of thinking is controlled by fear, feelings and excuses.

Joshua 1:8 urges us to base our thinking on godly counsel through meditation. Meditation entails engaging our minds on the issues of life with the word and counsel of God, in order to receive guidance and solution.

Meditation is from the Hebrew word "metalao." This

is a word used to describe how a class of animals called "ruminants" chew grass. Ruminants are animals such as cows, sheep, camels, etc. These animals have what we commonly refer to as pseudo (false) stomachs. They chew grass mainly as their food; but in the event that they find themselves in an environment where grass is not in ready supply, they have been designed to store unused grass in their pseudo stomach until when needed. These animals have the ability to regurgitate the stored grass and re-chew before swallowing it again.

This is similar to what happens in the process of meditation, where the word of God that has been read is recalled again and again. As you feed on the truth of God's word, you develop possibility mentality because you become what you behold.

Sometimes when you present a seemingly complex issue to some people, it is not unlikely that they say things like "I am going to go and chew on it" or "I will go and think (or sleep) on it." So, the whole essence of meditation is that you receive a big or complex idea and take it apart bit-by-bit, through meditative thinking.

When Moses sent twelve spies to survey the land that God had promised the Israelites will possess, ten of them came with a report that reflected a mindset of defeatism. Only Caleb and Joshua came back with a different report.

"And Caleb stilled the people before Moses, and said, Let us go up at once, and possess it; for we are well able to overcome it. But the men that went up with him said, We be not able to go up against the people; for they are stronger than we." (Numbers 13:30-31, KJV)

Although Joshua and Caleb were confronted with the same situation as others, they saw it differently, which affected their responses and actions. "We are well able." This was the mindset of Caleb and Joshua while others had the mindset that said "We are not able to possess the land."

THE GOD-CENTERED MINDSET

The response of Caleb and Joshua came from a mind that was wholly dependent on the ability of God. God testified of Caleb in Numbers 14:24:

"But my servant Caleb, because he had another spirit with him, and hath followed me fully, him will I bring into the land whereinto he went; and his seed shall possess it." (KJV)

Caleb had a mind that trusted in God. It is the kind

of mind that sees problems through strength and not weakness. Whereas the minds of the other Israelites that said "we are not able" only saw problems from their weaknesses, with little or no consideration for the ability of Jehovah.

Even though God had already given the Israelites victory over the giants and the land was theirs to possess, they placed limitations on themselves, based on wrong thinking of limitation, fear and doubt. Forty years later, they were still in the wilderness but now under the leadership of Joshua. The remaining of them were now ready to go in and posses the land. Joshua sent two spies to Jericho who were helped by Rahab (Joshua 2:1-11). Rahab told them about their enemy's opinion of them forty years earlier while they had been busy nursing fear and expressing unbelief. She said, "Forty years ago when you came out of Egypt, we heard reports about you and were scared of you and your God."

In one word, Rahab was simply saying that the land had been theirs to own forty years earlier. God had already gone ahead to remove the barriers but their mindset kept them back. That entire generation wandered for forty years in the wilderness and died, not embracing the plan of God. It was not because of the obstacle but because of a wrong mindset.

What are you faced with at this moment that looks like an insurmountable situation? If you have a word from God about it, I dare you to believe Him wholly and you will see that God is bigger than the situation. The barrier has been removed. Don't allow your mind to limit the ability of your unlimited God!

GROWING YOUR MIND

CHAPTER 7

GROWING YOUR MIND

In order to be victorious and effective in life, we must have a mind conditioned after the things that are superior - the things that are in alignment with God's word and purposes for our lives. This is because whenever a mind is set wrongly, it will continue to produce a life with wrong results. However, when a mind is conditioned after the word of God, it produces life and progress.

One of the remedies for a life of anxiety, panic and fear is developing a mind conditioned after the things of God. Philippians 4:6-8 counsels:

> *"Be anxious for nothing, but in everything by prayer and supplication, with thanksgiving, let your requests*

be made known to God; and the peace of God, which surpasses all understanding, will guard your hearts and minds through Christ Jesus. Finally, brethren, whatever things are true, whatever things are noble, whatever things are just, whatever things are pure, whatever things are lovely, whatever things are of good report, if there is any virtue and if there is anything praiseworthy - meditate on these things."

DEVELOPING A FAILURE-PROOF MINDSET

There are five ways you can develop a mindset that guarantees a continuously transformed life:

1. Embrace the mind of Christ. 1 Corinthians 2:16 says,

"For who hath known the mind of the Lord, that he may instruct him? But we have the mind of Christ." (KJV)

What was the mindset of Jesus that enabled Him to handle the affairs of life victoriously during His earthly ministry? How did He see and approach life? This we shall quickly consider, because knowing and embracing the mind of Christ will enable you to live victoriously. At redemption, you received the mind of Christ but it must be developed in order for you to continually enjoy triumphs in life.

There are four components of the mind of Christ that we must embrace in order to have a transformed mindset. The mind of Christ is scriptural, spiritual, wise, and humble.

- **Scriptural.** The mind of Jesus was rooted in the authority of the word of God. Throughout His earthly ministry, Jesus responded and acted in line with the word of God. Everything He did was in consonance with the word of God. He affirmed that everything He did was as commanded by the Father.

  Allowing your thinking and actions to be in alignment with the word of God will always guarantee a victorious outcome. Let your beliefs and actions be as commanded by God's word.

- **Spiritual:** The mind of Christ was spiritual. His mind and actions were as led by the Holy Spirit. He submitted to the guidance of the Holy Spirit. Men or circumstances cannot mislead you when the Holy Spirit leads you. You cannot misbehave in life when the Holy Spirit guides your actions (Romans 8:5-6).

- **Wise.** To be wise is to be supernaturally empowered to exercise discretion and sound judgment. It is to know what to do and say, and having the courage to do so. Mark 7:37 says that when people observed the ministry of Jesus, "… they were astonished beyond measure, saying, "He has done all things well. He makes both the deaf to hear and the mute to speak.""

Jesus exhibited a life of wisdom that kept even His enemies and adversaries amazed. He knew what to say, how to say it and where to say it. To this end, the Scripture enjoins us in Ephesians 5:15-16: "Be very careful, then, how you live - not as unwise but as wise, making the most of every opportunity, because the days are evil." (NIV)

Wisdom exercises sound judgment in speech and actions. It causes you to rise above every limitation and embrace the best you can be. With good wisdom, you will find that you are always on point on what to do, where to do it, with whom to do it and exactly how to do it. This is the wisdom that comes from God. When it rests on your mind, you possess a superior and undefeatable mind. Your mind grows as you embrace divine wisdom. Wisdom comes from God as you pray for it (James 1:5). Start praying for wisdom today.

• **Humble.** (Philippians 2:5). Humility is strength under control. It is the submission of your will to God's will, no matter how seemingly difficult it is to do so. The mind seeks to be independent of God's control and wants to be selfish. However, one of the ways the mind can be tamed is by being humbly submissive to God. We see this clearly demonstrated in the life of Jesus. In the Garden of Gethsemane, for example, He surrendered His will (the desires of His mind) to God by accepting to die on the cross.

2. **Take time to see your problem from a Bible hero point of view.** Apart from Jesus, who are your other heroes in the Bible? If they were in any situation comparable to where you are, how would they respond? If Apostle Paul was where you are now, how would he deal with the situation? How would Esther handle such a situation? How would Moses handle it? You must continually borrow from the mindsets of such people. And this will definitely grant you victory.

3. **Find someone who has solved the problem you are faced with and learn from them.** Do you know anyone in contemporary times or in your environment who has solved the same problem effectively and in a manner consistent with biblical views? Whenever I find myself confronted with

solving some problems, I have many times borrowed the mindsets of my mentors such as the late Kenneth E. Hagin or Bishop I.V. Hilliard. I usually ponder, "How would they handle a situation like this?" There are times that I would even hear their voices inside of my spirit.

4. **Read some books that address the solutions to your problem and summarize what you read.** Find an authority in that area and read their books for practical ideas and strategies.

5. **Find at least six promises in the Bible that speak to your situation and memorize them.** Locate what God's word has said concerning your situation. This will help you to know, declare and speak what God says in order for you to have good success. God told Joshua in Joshua 1:8:

> *"This Book of the Law shall not depart from your mouth, but you shall meditate in it day and night, that you may observe to do according to all that is written in it. For then you will make your way prosperous, and then you will have good success."*

Practicing all of the above will help you to develop the mindset of a champion.

THE EIGHT THINKING SKILLS OF EFFECTIVE PEOPLE

CHAPTER 8

THE EIGHT THINKING SKILLS OF EFFECTIVE PEOPLE

From my study of the lives of men and women who achieved extraordinary successes in their various endeavors, I have observed the following thinking skills:

1. REFLECTIVE THINKING

This is the ability to revisit the past, not for the purpose of regret but so you can gain a new perspective. When David was confronted with the giant, Goliath, in 1 Samuel 17, he remembered how God had helped him to kill a lion and a bear with his bare hands. Reflecting upon these past victories gave David the confidence and courage to face his current battle, which was Goliath. Knowing fully well that if he could kill a lion and a bear with his bare hands with the help of God and his skills, it was possible to defeat Goliath.

Reflective thinking helps you to know how you got to where you are, so you can gain a proper perspective of where you are going. Many people are usually discouraged and depressed in life because they focus mainly on the current difficulties facing them. One of the ways to prevail in such situations is by reflecting on your past victories over similar situations. By so doing, you will gain strength and courage to overcome any current challenge. If God has helped you in the past to overcome a similar situation, He will surely help you to overcome the current situation.

Hebrews 13:8 tells us clearly that "Jesus Christ is the same yesterday, today, and forever." God is an unchanging God. What He helped you to accomplish once can be accomplished over and over again, even under totally different conditions. This is why Psalms 103:2 counsels us not to forget His benefits. You must however be reflective in order to be thankful.

2. PROGRESSIVE THINKING

Many are stuck on one spot in life because of retrogressive thinking and outdated ideas. Making progress demands that you train your mind to be able to handle new and big ideas. It is impossible to make progress in life with a weak mind (Philippians 2:5). Weak minds are microscopic in operation. They only see and magnify small things - they never perceive big things.

If you take a microscope and focus it on a tiny spot, it will blow it up. Some people make issues out of nothing. You cannot be a success with your life if you think that way. There are so many people who are not making progress in life and are putting the blame on others. Some either put the blame on racial discrimination, societal injustice or even inadequate resources.

When you are fond of giving excuses in life, you will hardly make progress. We live in a rapidly changing world and progress demands that you continue to feed your mind with new ideas and contemporary knowledge.

Alvin Toffler once said, "The illiterate of the 21st

Century will not be those who cannot read and write, but those who cannot learn, unlearn, and relearn." This profound remark reveals three dimensions to change: You learn new truths, you unlearn what you used to know and you relearn what will help you to make progress.

There is a story of a young man who went fishing. Whenever he caught a fish, he would measure the fish with a stick. If the fish was shorter than or was the same size with the stick, he would drop it into a bucket. However if the fish was longer than the stick, he threw it back into the river. When his friend asked him why, he explained that the stick was the measurement of his frying pan at home; hence, any fish longer than the stick could not fit into his frying pan and was considered a waste.

This is an example of how the human mind operates. Whenever an idea comes that the mind does not have the capacity to contain, the mind repels it. So, unless your mind has been trained and fed with novel ideas, you may reject the very thing that may facilitate your progress. It is even possible to fight those who are trying to help you to your next level simply because your mind cannot comprehend what they are doing to help you.

3. CREATIVE THINKING

Creative thinking is applying Holy Spirit-inspired thoughts to create relevant solutions to the challenges of life. Creative thinkers usually think about something that does not exist and create it. Or they look at something already existing and improve on it. So, creative thinking can also be said to be finding new ways of doing old things.

However, creating new meaningful ideas and methods will require you to transcend traditional ideas and patterns. Jesus thought differently from the religious leaders of His time. His thinking was creative and radical, with outstanding results.

There is no challenge that you will encounter that has no solution. Psalms 90:2 says of God's foreknowledge:

"Before the mountains were brought forth, Or ever You had formed the earth and the world, Even from everlasting to everlasting, You are God."

God, who is the solution to every challenge of life, has been in existence prior to the emergence of any problem. Genesis 1:1 says that, in the beginning, Elohim, out of nothing, created. God is a creative

God. And you also have been created with the ability to think creatively because you receive the creative ability of God at redemption.

By establishing a relationship with God through salvation, you are a partaker of the same intellectual capacity with God. Every child of God is a partaker of the mind that was behind the whole of creation (1 Corinthians 2:16). What a glorious position and privilege!

Armed with this knowledge and awareness, you are able to put your mind to work creatively. If you try an approach or idea and it does not work, sit down and connect with God in meditation so you can receive fresh ideas.

As a creative thinker, you don't wait for things to happen; instead, you challenge your mind, environment and resources to make things happen. Instead of thinking just like everyone else on a particular subject, think outside of the box. It was Steve Jobs who said, *"The people who are crazy enough to think they can change the world are the ones who do."*

Don't agree with the status quo. Strive to be relevant and utilize tools that can help your business or career. Whatever you are doing, think of how to be locally and globally relevant. The whole world has become one entity and one market.

4. INQUISITIVE THINKING

This is the art of asking meaningful and necessary questions. Until you question the regulars of life, nothing ever changes. Those who don't ask meaningful and necessary questions are usually conditioned by their environment.

There is this adage where I come from that 'Those who ask questions never get lost on the way." I challenge you to boldly begin to ask necessary, wise questions from today. Don't allow your environment to condition you. The disciples asked Jesus a question in Matthew 17:19: "Why could we not cast it out?" In other words, how come we failed in the assignment given?

I was once told a story of a boy who wondered why his mother always cut the thighs and wings of a turkey before putting it in the oven. The woman replied that that was the way her own mother had taught her. When next they visited the grandmother, the boy asked her the question. To his surprise, the grandmother said her own mother too had taught her to always cut the thighs and wings of the turkey before putting it in the oven.

Since the great grandmother was alive, the boy asked her the same question as soon as he got the opportunity. The great grandmother replied that the ovens they had back in those days were too small to hold a whole turkey; so they had to cut the thighs and the wings to allow the turkey fit into the oven. She also added that no one did that in recent times because there were better and bigger ovens. Unknown to her, both her daughter and her granddaughter still kept the practice because they failed to ask necessary questions.

One of the ways to succeed in any given task is to ask relevant questions including but not limited to, "What do I need to do?" "Who do I need to assist me?" "Where do I need to go to obtain resources?" "What is it or who is it that I do not need around me at this time?"

5. FOCUSED THINKING

Lack of focus is one of the greatest enemies of success. Focused thinking is the ability to think clearly about a particular issue without distraction. It can also be said to mean being able to think clearly about an issue until you get a resolution. Since there are several distractions all around, it is very important that you remain focused, without responding to everything that you see. This will help you to channel your energy properly and not be dissipated.

Focused thinking is also the ability to prioritize the events of your life; being able to determine what is most important at each particular time. It is possible for several things to be competing for your time, but you must prayerfully decide what is the most urgent and the least urgent. Give yourself and your time to the most urgent and spend less time with the least urgent. This will help you not to major on the minors of life.

Focused thinking also involves determining who gets your time and attention. In Mark 1:35-37, the disciples came to tell Jesus that multitudes were seeking to meet with Him after seeing the various miracles that He had done in their town. In response, Jesus simply instructed the disciples in verse 38, that they should move to the next town. He remained focused on His divine assignment, without allowing the accolades of the people to keep Him grounded in one place.

Focused thinking also involves being vigilant. We sometimes lose our victories due to lack of vigilance or lack of sensitivity. Vigilance means not allowing any careless moment in your life or refusing to give room to distractions. In Songs of Solomon 5:2-8, there is the sad narrative of a damsel who missed the chance to be with her beloved due to lack of spiritual vigilance. You must be vigilant and alert so that God's plan for your life will be accomplished.

How does one develop a focused-thinking life? Learn to retreat and set yourself apart, so you can devote enough time to analyze and address whatever issue it is that is confronting you.

There are two things that keep you focused. The first is to define your desired end. If you don't know where you are going, any road will look like it. During His earthly ministry, Jesus was very focused in the pursuit of His assignment because He knew the reason why He came. He always kept his gaze and priority on His assignment and refused to be distracted. In John 4:34, He declared, "My meat is to do the will of him that sent me, and to finish his work." Also in John 17:4, He says, "I have glorified thee on the earth; I have finished the work, which thou gave me to do."

The case of Elisha too (in 2 Kings 2) is very instructive. When Elijah, his master, was to be taken to heaven, Elisha followed him fully to the end and received a double portion of his spirit because he knew what he wanted and remain focused. At every point that Elijah urged him to stay back from following him, he replied, "As the Lord lives, and as your soul lives,

I will not leave you!" Even in the face of provocation by the sons of the prophet, Elisha remained focused on the desired end of receiving the double portion of Elijah's spirit.

The second thing that helps your focus is to "count your eggs before they are hatched." This may sound contrary to the popular adage but it is a very potent strategy in this context. Hebrews 12:1-3 reveals to us that Jesus was able to endure the shame and pain of hanging on the cross because He kept His mind focused on the joy that lay ahead. What was the joy? The benefit that would result from dying on the cross; the benefit of seeing humanity delivered from the oppression of sin and darkness.

In the race of life, you are able to succeed when you don't focus on the pain but on the benefits that will accrue when you go through with the process.

6. STRATEGIC THINKNG

This is the ability to come up with plans of action that will produce great results for the future. It is the ability to chart a course of action on how to move from where you are to where you are going.

Apostle Paul said of himself:

"Therefore I do not run like someone running aimlessly; I do not fight like a boxer beating the air." (1 Corinthians 9:26, NIV).

Strategic thinking is usually proactive and not reactive. Proverbs 30:24-25 talks about ants, which despite being feeble, prepare their meat in the summer. The ants strategically anticipate a time of dryness and act to store food in order to prevent being in lack during winter. Strategic thinking causes you to anticipate challenges and provides strategies to prevent their occurrence. This gives you a competitive advantage in life.

As someone who wants to stay on top of life's challenges, your mind should be always be action-oriented. Don't just think about a problem - think about the actions to fix it. When others are fixated about limitations, you should be thinking of solutions; you should be plotting a map with which to navigate the way out.

In the rebuilding of the wall of Jerusalem, Nehemiah had a strategy-focused approach (Nehemiah 2:11-17). His first approach was not to commence the job; rather, he first surveyed the environment in order to have a proper assessment of the problem at hand. This helped him to know the resources needed to accomplish the job, the challenges and the risk involved in tackling the job.

I have counseled many people that failed in business because they rushed into it with wrong assumptions. By asking them necessary questions, it was obvious that they jumped into such ventures with little or no strategies of succeeding. Some simply saw others doing something and they thought they too could do it.

Are you a businessperson? Think strategically about your business. Are you a student? Think strategically about your academic career. Strategize on how to move from where you are to where you are supposed to be. Are you employed in a workplace? Strategize on how to climb higher on your job.

7. POSSIBILITY THINKING

This is a form of thinking that keeps your hope alive despite the challenges you are confronted with. No one succeeds in life with defeated and hopeless thinking. In Mark 9:23, *"Jesus said unto him, If thou canst believe, all things are possible to him who believes."*

At the onset of an assignment, never tell yourself it cannot be done. The "I can't" mentality kills initiative faster than any other factor. Caleb and Joshua had a possibility spirit. Even in the face of contradictory evidences and the presence of the giants, they resolutely believed that it was possible to possess the land In Numbers 13:30, they said:

"...Let us go up at once, and possess it; for we are well able to overcome it." (KJV)

Possibility thinking says, "No matter what happens, I know that the outcome will be favorable." This is the type of thinking that helps you rise above the obstacles and challenges militating against your destiny.

You can only strategize for victory when you are fully convinced that there is a way out. Whatever you don't attempt, you cannot attain. It is interesting to note that while others in his generation died in the wilderness through unbelief, Caleb was still ready to fight and possess his inheritance even at 85 years of age. He declared to Joshua, the new leader of Israel:

"And now, behold, the Lord has kept me alive, as He said, these forty-five years, ever since the Lord spoke this word to Moses while Israel wandered in the wilderness; and now, here I am this day, eighty-five years old. As yet I am as strong this day as on the day that Moses sent me; just as my strength was then, so now is my strength for war, both for going out and for coming in. Now therefore, give me this mountain of which the Lord

spoke in that day…" (Joshua 14:10-12).

Possibility thinkers don't rest on their own abilities but anchor their hope and trust in the ability of God - knowing that whatever He has promised, He is faithful to perform.

There is also a striking account of Abraham's encounter with God in Genesis 15:3-5:

> *"Then Abram said, "Look, You have given me no offspring; indeed one born in my house is my heir!" And behold, the word of the Lord came to him, saying, "This one shall not be your heir, but one who will come from your own body shall be your heir." Then He brought him outside and said, "Look now toward heaven, and count the stars if you are able to number them." And He said to him, "So shall your descendants be."*

Abraham started talking to God while inside the tent. He complained that God had not given him an offspring. There is something significant here. Being in the tent signifies a position where your only focus is on what you lack. In other words, you only have a limited and limiting view when inside of the tent. You're limited to what you can see within the confines of the tent. The "tent" here can be your race, ethnicity, culture, city, or your circle of friends. As long as you stay in that tent, you will only see and interpret life by its dimensions.

In order to embrace the fulfillment of the promise, God had to bring Abraham outside of the tent to reinforce his faith. Inside the tent, all Abraham could see were his challenges and limited resources but God took him outside of the confinement for a better view. When brought outside, he had an unrestricted vision of unlimited possibilities. God instructed him to look up and count the stars even inside the darkness. No matter how dark your situation is, there are shining stars. Don't focus on the darkness but on the stars in the darkness.

God instructed Abraham to count the stars. He was to count his opportunities even within the dark hour. Physically, it meant that he should look beyond his immediate environment; but spiritually, it meant that he should look beyond his resources and focus on God.

Stop looking at yourself from the tent and begin to look up outside of the tent. Stop looking at others for help and focus on God and the stars hiding inside the darkness. Focus on the opportunities hiding inside the problem!

8. GENERATIONAL THINKING

God is a generational thinker and everything he does has generational impact. When God blesses you, it has generational consequences and God expects you to pass it on from one generation to another.

Looking through the scriptures, there is a consistent pattern of how God related to people with their subsequent generations in mind. In Genesis 13:14-15, we're told:

> *"And the Lord said to Abram, after Lot had separated from him: "lift up your eyes now and look from the place where you are - northward, southward, eastward, and westward; for all the land which you see I give to you and your descendants forever."*

God's covenant blessings with Abraham were not just for him but also for his descendants. The Bible also has it that when Abraham paid tithes to Melchizedek, the Levites, who were Abraham's descendants, paid tithes in Abraham's loins. (Hebrews 7:8-10).

Proverbs 13:23 says that *"A good man leaves an inheritance for his children's children. But the wealth of the sinner is stored up for the righteous."*

A generational thinker thinks beyond his personal needs because he knows that his life is not just about him but about the generations after him. A generational thinker is one who carries the seed of the future on his shoulder. Effective people think generationally and not parochially. They think investment and not consumption.

In everything you do, think of how the generation after you can be better off than you, not worse off. This is what is called "The big picture" thinking - thinking beyond yourself and your immediate environment.

Short-term thinkers don't think of the big picture; they only focus on immediate gratification. One of the qualities of a mature or effective person is preference for delayed gratification. In the business world, this is called system thinking - understanding that other people's lives are tied to your choices.

A generational thinker must plan for at least four generations ahead.

BECOMING A NEW YOU: DEPROGRAM TO REPROGRAM

CHAPTER 9

BECOMING A NEW YOU: DEPROGRAM TO REPROGRAM

"And no man putteth new wine into old bottles: else the new wine doth burst the bottles, and the wine is spilled, and the bottles will be marred: but new wine must be put into new bottles" (Mark 2:22, KJV)

Are you bound to a life of addiction to destructive substances, such as alcohol or drugs? Or do you have any destructive habits? Do you desire a change in any area of your life?

At whatever level you are right now, there is a

newer and better level awaiting you. A new you can emerge through a "new mind transplant." The current mindset cannot take you to your next level. Getting to a new level requires a total makeover of your person by making over your mind.

MILITARY EXAMPLE

When you enlist in the military, they begin your training by putting you through what is called "boot camp." During that period, you're completely deprogramed. Your hair is cut and you get a uniform so you can have the unique look of a soldier. You are taught to salute; and you're taught to respond to your superiors in certain ways and to obey commands instantly even though you may not understand why.

In essence, they deprogram you and then reprogram you to think and act effectively and efficiently as a courageous member of the armed forces.

To apply this practically, embracing a life of liberty and continuous breakthrough requires a similar process of deprograming to be reprogramed. In the words of Jesus, quoted at the beginning of this chapter, in embracing a new life, which is the new wine, the old mindset must be replaced with a newer one.

THE THREE COMPONENTS OF MAN

For total transformation to take place, there must be an understanding of the components of man. 1 Thessalonians 5:23 reveals that every human is a tripartite being with three components: the spirit, the soul and the body. You are first a spirit, possessing a soul and housed inside a physical body.

The challenge of thinking and acting correctly lies in the ability of the spirit to control the soul and the body. The soul of man comprises the mind, the will and the emotion; while the body functions through the five senses of sight, smell, taste, hearing and feeling.

Real development takes place in the area of the mind. So the makeover process focuses on the maturity of the soul. Romans 12:1-2 says,

> *"I beseech you therefore, brethren, by the mercies of God, that ye present your bodies a living sacrifice, holy, acceptable unto God, which is your reasonable service. And be not conformed to this world: but be ye transformed by the renewing of your mind, that ye may prove what is that good, and acceptable, and perfect, will of God."* (KJV)

The world, through its system of media, education,

art, music, fashion, government, ideas and philosophies, always seeks to press the believer into its mode. And the gateway or the battleground is the mind. The believer's challenge, therefore, is how to not conform to the dictates of this world but to be transformed by the renewing of their minds.

At the point of redemption, only the spirit of the believer is regenerated; his mind remains unchanged until a renewing process takes place. 1 Corinthians 2:12 says, "We have not received the spirit of the world but the spirit of God that we might know the things that are freely given of God." This means that at the point of salvation, the mind receives the capacity to comprehend and absorb the salient truths of God's word that will facilitate its renewal and transformation.

THE RENEWAL PROCESS

The mind is like the storage system of the computer. The way a person thinks and acts come from the information, value system and ideologies that have been stored in the mind. In order to enjoy a life of continuous victory, the mindset of defeatism, fear, unbelief, doubt, inferiority, poverty and the likes must be deleted and replaced with a superior, godly mindset. This requires a renewal process or a deprogramming.

The renewal process inside of the mind is a gradual and progressive one. Before accepting Christ as a believer, you lived according to the dictates of the flesh emanating from the old Adamic nature. The old Adamic nature was sinful, depraved, selfish and ungodly. This is because the natural man possesses a natural mind - a mind that is governed and controlled by sin, Satan, and worldly philosophies. However, as the regenerated man begins to study, meditate on and apply God's word, the renewal process is activated and sustained.

As a believer who wants to continually walk in liberty and dominion, your mindset must be governed by a godly or biblical value system. You must learn to let your spirit man be the king, to let your soul be the servant and to let your body be the slave. The goal of this is for your will to become God's will, for your mind to become God's mind and for your emotions to respond as God would. In order for you to conquer and progress in life, you must bring your soul under the control and leadership of the Spirit of grace inside of you.

However, your soul can only become subject to the Spirit of God as you develop your spirit man. You cannot allow your emotions to drive and control you; rather, you must always yield to the leadership of the

Spirit. This is the maturity process and the seven steps below will boost the development of your spirit man to gain control over your mind.

1. Engage in fasting at least one day in a week. As I said before, fasting and prayer strengthens your spirit, and focuses your mind properly so it can gain ascendency over the body. Whenever you engage in fasting, your spirit and soul become more sharpened and alert to God and the things of God. Your spirit and soul are more empowered to control the body. So whatever stronghold of addiction, character flaws or weaknesses you are experiencing, keep rebuking and renouncing them as you fast and pray. The chains will break and grace will be released for you to rise higher.

2. Always walk in the awareness of your new position in Christ. The renewal of your mind demands that you have the revelation of your new position in Christ. Romans 6:9 says, "Knowing that Christ, having been raised from the dead, dies no more. Death no longer has dominion over Him."

Remain focused on the victory Christ won for you on the cross and refuse to be clouded by the secular culture around you. Identify with the newness of life in Christ. You have been crucified with Christ. Always walk in the awareness that you are a new person in

Him (Galatians 2:20).

3. Consistently seek to know God's will in every situation and consciously surrender yourself to it. Consciously commit your life to God each morning. You can even say it out aloud thus: "Today, I am going to live for you, Lord Jesus Christ."

My wife counseled a sister who had marital problems some years ago. While trying to get her to understand and submit to the will of God, the sister said to her, "In this case, Christianity apart, let us put the word of God aside." What she implied was that her Christianity was not ready to consider or submit to the word of God.

When your desire is to align every step you take with God's word, you cannot end up in a wrong destination. Are you tempted to think or act wrongly? Prayerfully make pleasing God your desire and He will direct all your paths. However this requires self-control because the greatest weapon for spiritual maturity is self-discipline. (Proverbs 16:32).

4. Spend time with God in prayer and the study of the Bible. 2 Corinthians 3:18 says, "But we all, with unveiled face, beholding as in a mirror the glory of the Lord, are being transformed into the same image from glory to glory, just as by the Spirit of the Lord."

You become what you behold. You take upon yourself the nature and character of the one you spend the most time with. Whosoever you behold is who you will ultimately become. Spending quality time in God's presence through prayer and His word makes you think and act like Him.

Are you confronted with any stronghold at this moment? Set at least one day aside in fasting weekly with the goal of gaining victory over the challenge. As you prayerfully spend time in studying God's word, the Holy Spirit changes you gradually to become a better vessel. The Holy Spirit will transform you into the image and the likeness of God as you continue this beholding process over a period of time.

Practicing the above step on a regular basis will definitely require discipline and determination because many things will compete for your time. But you must remain focused. Don't allow yourself to be discouraged even if you fail, get back up and keep on the regimen. Before long, you will see yourself conforming to God and His word.

5. Be in a relationship with at least one other person who can hold you accountable for spiritual growth. Find someone you can trust, someone you can relate to, who can hold you accountable for your spiritual growth. Invite him or her to take the spiritual journey with you. Jesus adopted this strategy for his disciples by constantly sending them in pairs and groups. The Scripture affirms that, *"As iron sharpens iron, So a man sharpens the countenance of his friend."* (KJV)

Note however that whoever you choose to partner with must be someone whose values align with your goal. It can also be a mentor or a colleague. Ecclesiastes 4:9-10 rightly says that,

> *"Two are better than one, Because they have a good reward for their labor. For if they fall, one will lift up his companion. But woe to him who is alone when he falls, For he has no one to help him up."*

By the grace of God, I have had the privilege of helping some men overcome addiction to pornography because they confided in me. I remember vividly a young man who had just graduated from college who was hooked up on watching pornography and engaging in masturbation daily. He confided in me and I gave him the permission to call me whenever he was tempted, no matter the hour of the day. This he did for a while. Today, he is totally free, to the glory of God.

When you keep your secret a secret, the devil and your flesh will use it to defeat you. You must of course be careful to allow only trusted and mature persons into your secret - those who can maintain confidentiality.

6. Never stop thinking of things that will strengthen your faith and sustain a positive mindset. Philippians 4:8 says: *"Finally, brethren, whatsoever things are true, whatsoever things are honest, whatsoever things are just, whatsoever things are pure, whatsoever things are lovely, whatsoever things are of good report; if there be any virtue, and if there be any praise, think on these things."*

Feed your mind with the things that are wholesome, pure, honest, good and lovely. Know that your eyes, ears and mouth are the gateways that feed information to your body. This means that what you watch, read, say and listen to all affect your mindset and ultimately your actions. You must therefore exercise discretion and discipline over these areas.

To be honest, many adults, especially parents, are more protective of what their children view than they are of their own minds and hearts – and yet they make decisions for themselves and their families. Instead of allowing wrong information into your heart, fill your heart daily with faith-filled words. Deliberately fill your heart with ideas and information on the next level you desire to attain.

7. Keep saying and doing those pure things you are thinking about. Constantly watch over your mouth in order to ensure that you continue to confess what you want and not what you feel. If your desire is abundance, don't speak lack. If you desire good health, think it and speak it. Don't desire good health and speak the vocabulary of sickness and disease over your life. Whatever you don't want in your life, eliminate it from your vocabulary.

Everything that exists came to existence by the word of God.

"By faith we understand that the worlds were framed by the word of God, so that the things which are seen were not made of things which are visible" (Hebrews 11:3).

Don't allow the pressures of life to cause you to speak lack, doubt, unbelief and fear. Rather, consistently and prayerfully speak positive words that are in alignment with your desired goal. With time, you will see your life becoming what you are thinking and saying.

I see you rising to the top in Jesus name!

Seven Potent Breakthrough
PRAYERS FOR OVERCOMING
Strongholds And Becoming A New You

Begin this prayer session by praising God for who He is. He is a faithful and compassionate God who does what He says. Thank God for the privilege to approach him in prayers and also for the great things that can be accomplished through prayers.

1. By the authority in the name of Jesus, I pull down every fortress and stronghold of darkness that has been established in my mind. I plead the blood of Jesus over my mind for complete deliverance and wholeness.

2. Whatever form of addiction or destructive behavior I am engaged in currently, I receive the power of the Holy Spirit from on high to shatter and break them away from me in Jesus Name. I revive the grace for self-control and the grace to master my ways of thinking and acting in Jesus name. From today and henceforth, I receive the grace to think and act in alignment with God's plan and purpose for my life. I rebuke any and

every force seeking to control me against my will in Jesus name.

3. I pray by the authority in the name of Jesus, that every unfruitful way of thinking operating in my mind be rebuked and removed. I decree in the name of Jesus that my mind is fruitful and progressive. From today and henceforth, wisdom for profitable living will continue to flow out of my mind like rivers of living water.

4. O God of heaven, let every old pattern of failure and old pattern of defeat be removed and destroyed from my life, and let new patterns that will bring my desired change be established in Jesus Name.

5. As rivers do not struggle to flow, and birds do not struggle to fly in the sky, I will never struggle to excel in life. By the authority in the name of Jesus, I will excel from one dimension to another.

6. 2 Kings 4:9. I perceived Elijah as a holy man. Whenever darkness covers a destiny, it is either the destiny will not be noticed or will be wrongly perceived. Many are loaded with potentials for greatness but are walking about unnoticed and undiscovered. By the power in the blood of Jesus, I command every form of darkness covering my

destiny to be removed now and forever. By the authority in the Name of Jesus, every wrong perception that has made people to ignore and shun my destiny is changed today. Those who are meant to help me will begin to perceive me rightly and shall embrace my destiny. I decree that my generation will embrace, receive and celebrate my God-given destiny in Jesus Name.

7. Acts 28:2. The barbarians showed Paul and his crew no little kindness. People who ordinarily don't show kindness showed too much kindness to Paul. A barbarian is a human who is perceived to be uncivilized, brutal, cruel, warlike, and insensitive. By the authority in the name of Jesus, I pray that from today, grace is granted unto me to begin to receive favor and kindness from unlikely sources, in Jesus Name.

THE GREATEST PRAYER
OF A LIFETIME

The greatest prayer of a lifetime is to be reconnected back to God in a living relationship. Relationship is the basis for asking. You cannot pray to a God whom you don't know and who does not know you. God wants to be intimate with you. This type of relationship is available to each one of us when we sincerely repent of our sins, and ask God's forgiveness, and receive His Son, Jesus, as our personal Lord and Savior. If you have never surrendered your life to God, or if you have turned away from God and you want to return to Him, now is the time. God is waiting for you. His arms are open wide to receive you. Just pray this simple prayer right now:

O Lord, be merciful to me, a sinner. I realize that I am a sinner. I need a savior and you are my savior. I repent of every sin, every wrongdoing, and I ask for your forgiveness. I receive Jesus Christ, Your only begotten Son, as my Lord and my Savior. I believe that Jesus went to the cross for me and paid the price for my salvation, and now I receive Him into my heart. I declare that I am born again. I am a child of God. Old sins are gone, and I have a brand-new life in Christ in Jesus' name. Amen.

I WOULD LOVE TO HEAR FROM YOU!

Thank you for purchasing this book. I would love to hear from you, but even more than that, I would love to pray for you and write back to you. I hope you will let me know what you are believing God for, so we can join together in agreement and turn our faith loose for miracles. I look forward to your testimony!

Send your prayer requests to me at:

Dr. Festus Adeyeye
Adeyeye Evangelistic Ministries (AEM)
P.O Box 810
West Hempstead, NY 11552
E-mail: aboluade@aol.com
Website: www.alccwinnershouse.org